LUNA GODDESS

That's What "THEY" Say

We Hear That Phrase All The Time Growing Up.
But What Does It Mean??

Change your life, and your life will change

Unknown

Contents

Preface

There's a reason "they" say the English language is the hardest to learn, (I still haven't figured out who "they" are but) in my opinion it's simply because we say the most ridiculous things. If we call someone a "Fuddy - duddy" we might get some crazy looks. What is a Fuddy-duddy?? Well, it's an old-fashioned term meaning; a foolish person. That term actually originated in the 19th century in the U.S.A.

~ Did you know that Janet irons her sheets. She's a real fuddy-duddy!

The reason I'm writing this book is two fold ;)

- I love to teach people things
- I love making people laugh and smile
- BONUS: I get to learn about what "They" are saying…

In this book I will be showing you some of my favorite quirky phrases. You will get to learn where that phrase originated from, what it means & I'll even use it in a sentence for you so it really makes sense! I will also give some of my own thoughts about the phases, Please remember they are just my own personal opinions.

I would hear all kinds of phrases that really didn't make a whole lot of sense as a child, they just became a part of our language.

However as a child I would get confused by the things people would say so I would always ask, "How do you know", their answer was always the same!
That's What "They" Say

As I got to be in my 20's and 30's though I started to think about how cool it would be to have a book with a bunch of these phrases in it. I thought "what a great way to make people laugh". I thought it would be an easy read, a great gift for the person who you never know what to buy for them or they just have everything already. It would be a great book to have sitting on your coffee table, in the bathroom for the guys to have something to do. No matter in what way it's used, one thing is for sure and that is it will be nostalgic!

I just want to say how proud I am of myself for writing this book. When I was in college for Photography, one of my classes I had to take was Photojournalism and to be honest it was the first time I was a bit worried about a class in school. Some things about me is that I'm very competitive, OCD & a perfectionist so in school I had to be the best. I worked my butt off in that class & after turning in my final exam my professor called me personally to tell me that I was just crazy if I didn't think I was a good writer. He told me that I could have my paper published just the way it was. Now I wish I had taken his advice but, the silver lining is that he made me feel really good about myself. Psst, I got an A+ of course ;)

One

Dedication

To my kids Nikoletta and Tristan, Thank you for ALWAYS believing in me, for always being by my side no matter what, for trusting in me to make the right decisions for us, for forgiving my mistakes, for your unconditional love and support you give to me every single day of my life.

The two of you are my rocks, you keep me sane & smiling with the crazy world around us. I know I'll never be alone because I'm blessed with the two of you! I feel like I won the lottery everyday because I have not only one but two of the kindest, most caring people with me everyday! I love you both more than I can ever express!

~ Mom

P.s. Love to our two beautiful fur babies Artemis & Isis

P.s.s Shout out to all my Posh Friends (Family), you all have given me so much strength.

~ To ALL of my ex's HA! I told you I was going to write a book like this one day! Enjoy the read!

Nikoletta - Myself - Tristan

Artemis - Isis

Two

Fun Quotes

"Optimist: someone who figures that taking a step backward after taking a step forward is not a disaster, it's more like a cha-cha."
  - Robert Brault

"I believe that if life gives you lemons, you should make lemonade… And try to find somebody whose life has given them vodka, and have a party."
  - Ron White

"Nothing is impossible, the word itself says "I'm possible!"
  - Audrey Hepburn

"When tempted to fight fire with fire, remember that the Fire Department usually uses water."
  - Unknown

How do you get a sweet little 80-year-old lady to say the F word? Get another sweet little 80-year-old lady to yell "BINGO!"

Anonymous

I dream of a better tomorrow, where chickens can cross the road, and not be questioned about their motives.

Anonymous

Why do people say "no offense" right before they're about to offend you?

Anonymous

"Knowledge is when you learn something new every day. Wisdom is when you let something go every day."

-Ralph Waldo Emerson

I can take it. The tougher it gets, the cooler I get.

Richard M. Nixon

I want to be a vampire. They're the coolest monsters.

Gerard Way

Three

35 Idioms & a Bonus

#1 STUPID-O CLOCK

Meaning: Very early in the morning or Very late at night, depending on the way <u>you</u> look at it.

Originated: In Britain, in the late 20th Century

How to use it: Yesterday we went to watch the sunset, then we rushed to the beach to watch the moon rise. We were having so much fun taking pictures before we knew it, it was stupid-o clock.

My Thoughts: I hadn't heard this one before but it's a great way to say you home late AF. (lol) See what I did there and didn't even mean to. I might be 46 but I'm still up on the younger generations lingo, well for the most part anyways.

* * *

#2 BITCH SLAP

Meaning: An open-handed slap in the face intended to be humiliating.

Originated: USA, In the late 20th Century (of course that one would be from here) lol

How to use it: DAMN, he straight up bitch slapped his ass.

My Thoughts: Ok, growing up in this era I am not surprised that this phrase comes from here. When rap and r&b hit it big in the 90's, MTV Videos was awesome, it actually had the videos of the songs, so if you didn't hear that term that's only because you weren't born yet

* * *

#3 ONCE IN A BLUE MOON

Meaning: A very rare occurrence

Originated: Britain, 19th Century

How to use it: What do you mean she cleaned her room without being asked?? That has to be a once in a blue moon occurrence.

My Thoughts: The blue moon is a rare occurrence, it only happens when there are two full moons in the same month leading to the following month, not having a full moon in any given month is called the Blue Moon!

* * *

#4 RIDING SHOTGUN

Meaning: To be riding in the front seat of a vehicle.

Originated: USA made, mid 20th Century, it says it was initially heard in cowboy film?!?

How to use it: I can't drive so I'm riding shotgun.

My Thoughts: I don't know anything about cowboy films so I can't comment on that. However I can tell you the way it works. Let's say you are going on a road trip with some friends, once you all can see the car you have to yell "SHOTGUN", the 1st person that does gets the front seat! It was always a fun unspoken thing, well fun for the person who gets the front seat ;)

* * *

#5 HOLY SHIT

Meaning: An expression of extreme surprise or disbelief

Originated: USA made 100%

How to use it: Holy Shit Mark won the lottery two times! That's got to be next to impossible or once in a blue moon. ;)

My Thoughts: I grew up saying this all the time. Probably more than

I should have. Sometimes I don't think people know what to initially think about me because swearing is just simply part of my vocabulary. They are just words, people! I honestly don't even realize how much I actually swear/curse.

* * *

#6 BREAK A LEG

Meaning: A superstitious way to wish "good luck" to someone before a performance or game while avoiding saying "good luck" out loud, which is considered unlucky.

Originated: USA, 20th Century

How to use it: His mom always says break a leg before he plays, but he doesn't need it. He's got this!

My Thoughts: Honestly I'm not a superstitious person but even if I was, I just felt that saying break a leg to someone as "good luck" did not sound right at all! Even now after finding out why people say it, I still think it's a confusing statement. I'd bet that most people just say it because that's what they grew up hearing not because they are superstitious. Remember these are just my opinions.

* * *

#7 BARKING UP THE WRONG TREE

Meaning: Responding to something that isn't the important issue

Originated: Britain, 19th century

How to use it: The government is blaming the immigrants for the banking crisis, but they are barking up the wrong tree there.

My Thoughts: Ok, yes I know of this phrase but it took me way too long to come up with a sentence to use as an example to ever see a use for it in my life. Nope, I still can't think of a time I would want to say that phrase.

* * *

#8 SAVED BY THE BELL

Meaning: Saved by a last second intervention of some kind.

Originated: Britain, 18th century. Not connected, as often thought to the phrase, to bells attached to coffins.

How to use it: Shannon almost got his ass chewed out by his wife, but was saved by the bell when the doorbell rang.

My Thoughts: I love this one, I have said it sooooo many times in my life. To be honest that sentence actually happened to me. Lol I have said that so many times in relationship situations. I'm sure at least some of you can relate.

* * *

#9 SKELETON IN THE CLOSET

Meaning: A secret, usually something that you are ashamed of and don't want anyone to find out about.

Originated: The United Kingdom, in Britain they say Cupboard but in the USA we still say Closet

How to use it: The guy that lives down the hall was convicted of child neglect. I wonder what other skeletons he has in his closet, he always looks sketch to me!

My Thoughts: I feel that by the time you are an adult, if you don't own some skeletons then you are just not living life to its fullest. I can't speak for everyone but in my opinion not all skeletons are bad, maybe just embarrassing. Here's one of mine. The last time I spoke to the nut job that raised me, I was as mad as a hatter and I don't regret a single word!

* * *

#10 MAD AS A HATTER

Meaning: Someone who's crazy or prone to unpredictable behavior

Originated: 17th century, linked to the hat-making industry and mercury poisoning. It turns out that the process they used to make their hats was poisoning them and driving them insane. It wasn't until 1941 that the hatters discovered what was causing them to behave so strangely.

How to use it: Andy was mad as a hatter when his truck broke down.

My Thoughts: Honestly when I hear any term that sounds like "The mad hatter" I think of Alice in wonderland. However, I'm glad I picked this one because I had no idea about the hatters! That really sucks. We are all lucky to be living in a time where we have already figured out that lead and mercury are not good for us.

* * *

#11 BASKET CASE

Meaning: A failing person or thing, unable to function properly.

Originated: US Military, immediately following WWII. Originally this referred to soldiers who had lost arms and legs and had to be carried in a basket!

How to use it: The war caused so many basket cases.

My Thoughts: WTF! I had no idea that this term was so terrible. I really hope this is not true. I can't even imagine using that term in that way. To me it just means someones being crazy. What do you guys think?

***

#12 CUT THE CHEESE

Meaning: To expel international gas. Fart, break wind

Originated: Not known for sure but it appeared around the 1950's - 1970's depending on who you want to believe. Using the word cheese is because there are many types of cheese that don't have a great odor to them.

How to use it: Yesterday at the beach Mark told everyone to back up because he just cut the cheese.

My Thoughts: Not that the term itself bothers me but, in my first marriage my husband didn't care at all who he was around or where he was, at least that's what it seemed like to me, when he would cut the cheese. But it's a bodily function, not much you can do about it. Holding in your farts is actually not healthy, but in my opinion if it's happening ALL the time then you need to look at what you are eating because cutting the cheese all the time is just too much! Think about your poor wife or girlfriend & please never ask her to "pull your finger" lol.

** * **

#13 A DIME A DOZEN

Meaning: It means that something is pretty common and almost worthless

Originated: USA, 20th Century

How to use it: The chairs in the lobby are nice but they're a dime a dozen.

My Thoughts: Honestly, I don't have much to say about this one because I didn't find anything very interesting about it. I'm not saying it's a bad phrase, just not one that I see myself using.

* * *

* * *

#14 HOLDING A CANDLE TO SOMETHING

Meaning: A way to describe a person or thing that is distinctly inferior to someone or something else. Often used in a negative to mean the opposite.

Originated: 16th century, apprentices used to be expected to hold the candle so that the more experienced workmen could see what they were doing. Meaning that was all they were capable of doing. - So mean

How to use it: Shannon is a good tattoo artist but he doesn't hold a candle to his own sons!

My Thoughts: If you can use this phrase in a positive way I'd like to hear it. This is just a great way to talk shit but say something nice at the same time. Lol It's kind of like a "double edge sword", because even though you are saying something nice about one person you are at the same time being mean to another.

* * *

#15 ACHILLES' HEEL

Meaning: Weak spot or vulnerable

Originated: The legend is ancient but wasn't picked up until the 19th century. - This comes from the myth (I am Not calling it a myth, "They" are) of Achilles, he was dipped into the river Styx by his mother Thetis to make him invulnerable. Unfortunately his heels didn't get covered by the water & he was later killed by an arrow wound to his heel.

How to use it: Sean will never be able to move on after the break up, she's his achilles heel.

My Thoughts: I just want to say that I love the movie about Achilles & I will admit I cried when he died; I am an Aries, leave me alone! Lol Also in case you are wondering, the connection between Achilles & heels is because the tendon at the back of a human heel was named the Achilles' tendon. If you didn't know that, you learned something new today!

* * *

#16 TO USE A SLEDGEHAMMER TO CRACK A NUT

Meaning: Using stronger measures than are really necessary to solve a problem.

Originated: USA, 1850's

How to use it: All they were doing was peacefully protesting, why did there have to be such a large police presence. It was like using a sledgehammer to crack a nut.

My Thoughts: Another one I have never heard of & even though I now understand what it means, I still won't use it most likely. Mostly because it's pretty long & in my opinion pretty weird.

* * *

#17 RED RAG TO A BULL

Meaning: Something that will cause an angry or violent reaction, it's intended to deliberately provoke someone else into reacting negatively.

Originated: 17th century, to wave a red rag at someone just meant to chat with them - 'red rag' was then slang for the tongue. Later in the 17th century the red rag was used as a distraction on animals. The first animal it was used on was the stupidest of birds, the pheasant. Bulls weren't added to the list until 1873.

How to use it: 1. Shut your piehole & give your redrag a break. (example for chatter) 2. Just mentioning his ex-wife's name was like a red rag to a bull, he gets so angry!

My Thoughts: I have heard this a lot in my life so it's not new to me. I can't say I have ever really used it in a sentence though. Instead ~ Quick trivia, Bulls can't distinguish the difference in colors, they don't have the optical equipment, I guess they just don't like a cloth being used to piss them off.

* * *

#18 WHEN HELL FREEZES OVER

Meaning: Simply means that something will never happen. Nope, not ever!

Originated: USA 19th century, Shocker!

How to use it: I will talk to her again when hell freezes over!!

My Thoughts: Yup, I've used this one many times! But with climate change, do you think it's possible that it *could* freeze over?? Jokes people, just jokes!

* * *

IT'S RAINING CATS AND DOGS

Meaning: A heavy downpour, rain coming down very fast and hard.

Originated: England 17th century, the city streets were filthy then and heavy rain would occasionally carry along dead animals.

How to use it: There's no way you guys are going to the park, it's raining cats and dogs outside.

My Thoughts: I'm not very satisfied with how it originated. I am a big cat lover. I live in CA now but when I lived in WI (I really miss the storms there, I love listening to the rain) and it would be storming outside my poor cat would be terrified, he would always be hiding under something and would never respond to us calling for him. Poor Cloudy, miss you :(

* * *

#20 GOING POSTAL

Meaning: To become crazed and violent, especially as the result of high stress in a workplace.

Originated: USA 1980's, A United States Postal Worker shot a total of 20 co-workers before killing himself. 14 people died in the attack. It's still the deadliest among incidents of violence in the workplace.

How to use it: Be Careful with that guy, I can see him going postal pretty easily.

My Thoughts: I was young when this happened, I remember watching it on the news. It was very sad and scary.The 80's wasn't even that long ago, things are so different now. Sorry no jokes about this one, I think I was just too close to it.

* * *

#21 AS HAPPY AS A CLAM

Meaning: It means to be very happy & content.

Originated: 19th century eastern USA, it sounds silly, how do we know if clams are happy? But if you look at a clam when it's open it looks like it is smiling.

How to use it: You made her happy as a clam with that birthday gift! She hasn't stopped smiling all day.

My Thoughts: There's a fuller version of this phrase, now rarely heard - 'as happy as a clam at high water'. You see high tide is when clams are free from the attentions of predators. That has to be their happiest time! I personally have not heard the full version before. I was just down at laguna beach the other day & I now can say that at night when high tide hits, it can get to be a bit scary. I know that makes me sound like a scaredy cat but, there are creatures in there. That is their home & I just don't think I should interrupt them. Lol My daughter though, completely the opposite, she just loves going to the beach. Maybe it's because she's a water sign & I'm a fire sign!

* * *

#22 A FOR EFFORT

Meaning: It's used when recognizing that someone tried hard to accomplish something although they might not have been successful at it.

Originated: USA 19th century, We all know in school the highest grade you can get is an A. Therefore if you give someone an A for effort (for doing something), you are accepting that they have tried even though they were unsuccessful.

How to use it: She worked all day making that dessert and then Jessica said it wasn't good. I give her an A for effort.

My Thoughts: This saying is nostalgic for me, even though it's not exactly the same phrase. My grandfather was the funniest guy, he always told the same jokes over and over but they were still funny. He would tell the kids he got all A's in school, Absent Absent Absent lol I miss the corny jokes grandpa ~RIP

* * *

#23 WHEN PIGS FLY

Meaning: It's a funny/ironic comment pointing out the unlikeliness of something happening

Originated: UK 19th century

How to use it: "I promise I'll clean my room tomorrow." "Sure when pigs fly."

My Thoughts: Now the literalists reading this all know that pigs can fly. Remember when "they" were all saying 'swine flu'! Hahaaha Just Jokes! I prefer 'When hell freezes over'. lol I think it makes a larger impact with what you are trying to say.

* * *

#24 WHIPPER SNAPPER

Meaning: Originally it refers to a younger person with no apparent get up and go, a know-it-all. Later it's changed to mean a young person with an excess of both ambition & impudence. lol

Originated: 17th century, This phrase actually merged with another phrase that already existed, a 17th century term for street rogues -

"snipper snappers", now known as 'whipper snapper'.

How to use it: Grandpa doesn't want a caregiver, he said he doesn't want some young damn whippersnapper coming over telling him what to do.

My Thoughts: I guess I had no idea what whipper snapper actually meant & from everything I read I'm not sure it's perfectly clear. In my opinion though from what I read, it's referring to a young person who thinks they are better than everyone else, basically I'd just say a brat!

* * *

#25 OVER THE MOON

Meaning: Extremely Happy, Delighted, Excited

Originated: 16th century. Although not widely used until the 1970's

How to use it: When I read Jose's card from our anniversary I was so over the moon!

My Thoughts: Personally, anything that has to do with the moon I love! I remember the nursery rhyme by Mother Goose, Hi diddle diddle, The Cat and the fiddle, The Cow jump'd over the Moon, The little dog laugh'd to see such craft, And the dish ran away with the spoon. ~Oh to be a kid again… On second thought, no thanks, to be a kid again for me would just plain SUCK! But for you young people out there, I know people are probably always telling you to "stop trying to grow up so fast". Seriously though, stop trying to grow up so fast, enjoy that your main responsibility is just going to school! I tell my kids that all the time, stop trying to do my job, you already have one it's called school!

* * *

#26 EVERY CLOUD HAS A SILVER LINING

Meaning: It's used to convey to someone that no matter how bad the situation might seem, there's always some good aspect to it.

Originated: 17th century

How to use it: Mom burned dinner again, but every cloud has a silver lining, now we get to order in.

My Thoughts: In my opinion, Mother Nature should get credit for this one. It's a fact that when clouds float in front of the sun they will sometimes have a "silver lining" around them. Just Saying. However I have another opinion, not to get all serious on ya but, this saying is true by its definition. Life will get bad at times, this I can guarantee but don't dwell on the negative, there's always something good that will come from it even if it's small.

* * *

#27 A PICTURE PAINTS A THOUSAND WORDS

Meaning: It is pretty literal, a picture expresses so much more than any amount of words.

Originated: 20th century, first written in 1911

How to use it: If you forget, use a picture, it paints a thousand words.

My Thoughts: I'm not happy with the little information I found about this saying, of course that's because I am a Photographer. That's what I went to college for. It doesn't matter how you say it, "paints, says, or worth a thousand words", a picture is priceless because it's a memory. Usually a good memory (I'm not talking about mug shots here) & it's a fact that our memories (in our brain) don't get better as time goes on, they get worse. However, look at a picture & the memory of the image will come flooding back to you! To me it is one of the most important things in life, pictures are always there to help you smile!

* * *

#28 JOSHING ME

Meaning: Someone is joking with you.

Originated: Late 1800's, when a kid named Josh Tatum noticed that the nickels minted in 1883 were so close to the same & design as the $5 gold pieces. He started to electroplate them and pass them off as $5 pieces. He made quite a bit of money until he got caught.

How to use it: Janet told me she was pregnant, I was so excited but it turns out she was just joshing me.

My Thoughts: I have used this term before, however in my opinion it's kinda dumb. I mean it's someone's name that's so common now. I'd rather use the phrase, screwing with me, messing with me or just be blunt and just say you're fu*king with me. I'm an adult and I can take it.

* * *

#29 YOU ARE WHAT YOU EAT

Meaning: It's a notion that to be fit and healthy you have to eat healthy food

Originated: <u>France</u>, 17th century but didn't hit America until the 1930's

How to use it: Did you know that "they" say 90% of diseases known to man are caused by unhealthy cheap junk foods? I guess you are what you eat.

My Thoughts: If my memory is correct, I remember hearing this used a lot when they made that movie about "fast food" & how it was the leading cause of obesity. I won't say which place I'm talking about but you know who you are! They have the best "<u>French</u>" fries but that's how they rope you in, don't fall for it people.

* * *

#30 HOCUS POCUS

Meaning: It's a magical charm that magicians used to say before they did a magic trick. It's a general term for magic or trickery. It's also the name of an awesome Halloween movie! (My oldest daughters favorite growing up)

Originated: Early 17th century, it started with comedy magicians using words like hocus pocus, abracadabra or shazam before they would do a trick. In the 1620's hocus pocus was used to describe conjurers (witches). If they were found to have actual magical powers then the witches were expected to have a grim, short future ahead of them.

How to use it: As Diane would say "That's just a bunch of hocus pocus".

My Thoughts: ~ Interesting to me~ The word Hocus is thought to be the source for the verb Hoax. However that doesn't appear until 1796, almost 200 years later, although the link seems intuitive, there's no direct evidence to link the two words. Must not be just Hocus Pocus!

* * *

#31 BALL AND CHAIN

Meaning: A 20th century slang term used in reference to a wife.

Originated: Both Britain and USA early 20th century. The allusion is the presumption that a man's wife must have held him back from the things he really wanted to do like, go to strip clubs, go to bars, sit around the house and do nothing if he wants to.

How to use it: "Wanna watch the game tonight"? "Yeah but, the ball and chain said she made dinner reservations".

My Thoughts: If you couldn't tell I really don't care for this term, I feel that it's degrading to us women. Not getting all feminist on you. I've been through enough in my life to know that most (not all) men are only held back by themselves! Also if they would learn to communicate better they would be much happier, you guys know what "they" say… Happy wife, Happy life! Jokes guys, just jokes ;) Kinda

* * *

#32 ROME WAS NOT BUILT IN A DAY

Meaning: It takes time to create great things, you can't expect success to come right away, with hard work and persistence you will get there.

Originated: Medieval France year 1190

How to use it: You keep doing the same thing and it's not getting you anywhere, slow down, take your time, Rome was not built in a day.

My Thoughts: This is a very true statement, "Rome was not built in a day," so slow down, be patient, and be persistent with your work. Success is just around the corner! ;) You can accomplish anything, you really can. However, in order to do that you have to believe in yourself, you have to like yourself, you have to love yourself and most importantly you have to be consistent with your actions!

* * *

#33 CHICK FLICKS

Meaning: A movie with characterizations and story-lines that appeal especially to women.

Originated: Early 1990's, However in the 1970's that term was know for sexual movies, like porn.

How to use it: "Sweetheart, can we watch Sleepless in Seattle tonight"?

"That sounds like a chick flick".

My Thoughts: I actually find it funny when guys try to act like they don't like movies that are labeled "chick flicks" because every time I have gotten a guy to watch one they always liked it! Always! You all know who you are too! You know what, just give one a try, you can even watch one when no ones around. Who will know? Stop worrying about what others think of you, your "guys" won't make fun of you. lol

* * *

#34 BROWNIE POINTS

Meaning: Basically Brownie Points is a way of figuring out where you stand with your woman - good or bad. This started way back in the leprechaun days, I guess that's long before they created "The Doghouse".

Originated: The way guys mean it when said now started in the 1940's

How to use it: Jose tells her he loves her, "I love you, I love you more than yesterday but not as much as tomorrow"! "You just scored a lot of brownie points.

My Thoughts: In my opinion if a guy or girl does something out of the blue that wasn't expected, then I guess saying "you got brownie points", is fine. I remember when the I love you quote above was said to me, it really did make me feel loved & happy. However to me it's not looked at as a points system. I look at it like "It's the little things that matter". I'm not the only one who says that either, "they" do too! ;)

* * *

#35 NEVER JUDGE A BOOK BY IT'S COVER

Meaning: You should never judge something or someone just by the way it looks on the outside.

Originated: Surprisingly this one is very recent, 1944

How to use it: I'm so glad she didn't judge a book by its cover, or she would have never married him.

My Thoughts: I felt this was a perfect one to end my first book with. I personally feel very strongly about judging. I never judge anyone. I strongly feel that everyone should be able to express themselves the way they feel and not have to be worried about what someone might think of them. I know that is an easy thing to hope for but sadly not what I see happening any time soon. It takes a long time to get the strength to not care what others think about you but trust me when I say, it can be done! I love meeting new people, all kinds of different people, I love learning from them. Everyone has special things about them, you just can't always see it from the outside.

* * *

BONUS - BAT SHIT CRAZY

Meaning: rude slang, Unreasonably or Uncontrollably wild, irrational, insane.

Originated: Not totally sure, from what I found it was around 1985

How to use it: Did you know that Gayle watched some video on how to clean your organs by using peroxide, so she drank peroxide. OMG, she is literally bat shit crazy!

My Thoughts: Are you wondering how I came up with such a strange question to use? Well I'm going to tell you either way, it's because it's 100% true! When I first moved out to CA, I was helping a lady for 10 long, very long months and she was insane. Anything she would watch on the internet she would believe so she really did drink peroxide, I called 911, she ended up just fine. So in my opinion the best way to describe her is Bat Shit Crazy! lol

Four

Conclusion

I Hope you all enjoyed reading my first book. My whole goal for wanting to write this book was to make people laugh. I hope I was able to put a smile on your face. In case you couldn't tell from my book, I have a pretty sarcastic personality! I wanted this book to be something that anyone who reads it smiles!

So if I did accomplish that goal and you smiled, I would be ever so grateful if you would leave me a 5 star review on Amazon. Until writing this book I didn't really realize how important it can be to write a review for someone's career.

~ I'll leave you with this last thought: - *Your income can grow only to the extent you do!*

Five

Resources

Ginger. (2022, January 1). *All Phrases.* Ginger Software. Retrieved May 21, 2022, from https://www.gingersoftwa re.com/content/phrase-of-the-day/page/1/

Farlex. (2003, January 1). *The Free Dictionary by Farlex.* Retrieved May 21, 2022, from https://idioms.thefreedictionary.com/hold+a+candle+ to

Martin, G. (1997, January 1). *The Phrase Finder.* Gary Martin. Retrieved May 21, 2022, from https://www.phrases.org.uk/index.html

About the Author

I'm not ashamed to say that I'm 46 years old. I'm a disabled single mother. We currently live in CA but we are originally from WI. Yup, a Midwest girl lives her whole life in Wisconsin & almost four years ago picks up and moves to California. There are reasons for that big change in our lives, but I won't get into that now. I plan to write a whole book about it. I've been an entrepreneur my whole life. While being a new writer, I also run three boutiques on poshmark.com, just look for moongoddess7 and moongoddessedgy depending on your style ;)

You can connect with me on:

🌐 https://poshmark.com/closet/moongoddess7